THE
FUNNIEST
& GROSSEST

≡ EVER! ≡

PORTABLE
PRESS

THE FUNNIEST & GROSSEST JOKE BOOK EVER!

is a compilation of the following two previously published titles:

The Funniest Joke Boke Ever! (ISBN: 978-1-62686-584-6)
The Grossest Joke Book Ever! (ISBN: 978-1-62686-585-3)

Portable Press
An imprint of Printers Row Publishing Group
10350 Barnes Canyon Road, Suite 100, San Diego, CA 92121
www.portablepress.com
e-mail: mail@portablepress.com

Printers Row Publishing Group is a division of Readerlink Distribution
Services, LLC. Portable Press is a registered trademark of Readerlink
Distribution Services, LLC.

All correspondence concerning the content of this book should be
addressed to Portable Press, Editorial Department, at the above address.

Publisher: Peter Norton
Associate Publisher: Ana Parker
Publishing/Editorial Team: Vicki Jaeger, Tanya Fijalkowski, Lauren Taniguchi
Editorial Team: JoAnn Padgett, Melinda Allman, Dan Mansfield
Production Team: Jonathan Lopes, Rusty von Dyl

Cover and interior concept by Patrick Merrell
Cover and interior by Tanya Fijalkowski

Library of Congress Cataloging-in-Publication Data

Names: Portable Press (San Diego, Calif.), author.
Title: The funniest & grossest joke book ever!
Other titles: The funniest and grossest joke book ever!
Description: San Diego, CA : Portable Press, [2017]
Identifiers: LCCN 2017006666 | ISBN 9781684121281 (pbk.)
Subjects: LCSH: Wit and humor, Juvenile. | Riddles, Juvenile.
Classification: LCC PN6166 .F86 2017 | DDC 818/.602--dc23
LC record available at https://lccn.loc.gov/2017006666

Printed in the United States of America

Second Printing: June 2017
21 20 19 18 17   2 3 4 5 6

What do you call a kid captured by a cannibal?

Stu!

What do you get when you cross a bear with a skunk?

Winnie the Pew.

When the moth hit the windshield,
what was the last thing to
go through its mind?

Its butt!

What do you call a cow with a twitch?

Beef jerky.

What do you call a hippy's wife?

Mississippi.

How does Darth Vader
like his toast?

On the dark side!

Q&A

If we breathe oxygen during the day, what do we breathe at night?

Nightrogen.

What's the hardest thing about learning to skate?

The ground!

What kind of bagel can fly?

A plain bagel.

Why shouldn't you write with a broken pencil?

It's pointless.

**Why couldn't the gnome
pay his rent?**

He was a little short.

What do you call a prehistoric pig?

Jurassic pork!

**Why is it dangerous to do math
in the jungle?**

Because if you add 4 and 4,
you get ate.

Why did dinosaurs walk so slowly?

Because running shoes hadn't
been invented yet.

Q&A

Why did the little strawberry cry?

Her mom and dad were in a jam.

Why did the rooster cross the road?

It was the chicken's day off.

What do you call a fake noodle?

An impasta.

Why don't zombies eat clowns?

They taste funny!

What do you give to a sick lemon?

Lemon aid.

Who makes the best
exploding underwear?

Fruit of the Boom!

What do you call a grizzly bear
caught in a rain shower?

A drizzly bear.

What kind of songs are
balloons afraid of?

Pop songs!

What is every magician's favorite
candy bar?

Twix.

What's white, furry, and shaped like a tooth?

A molar bear.

Did you hear about the computer program created by a chicken?

All you do is point and cluck.

What did the alpaca say when she was kicked off the farm?

"Alpaca my bags!"

What's the most important rule for doing science experiments?

Never lick the spoon.

What would bears be without bees?

Ears!

What do you give a seasick monster?

Plenty of room!

Why did the cowboy ride the bull?

It was too heavy to carry.

Which Great Lake do ghosts like best?

Lake Eerie.

Why do the French eat snails?

Because they don't like fast food.

**How did the frozen chicken
cross the road?**

In a shopping bag.

What do you call a rabbit with fleas?

Bugs Bunny.

**If athletes get athlete's feet,
what do astronauts get?**

Missile toe!

**Why can't you hear a pterodactyl
going to the bathroom?**

Because the "p" is silent.

**What do you get when you cross
a goat with a squid?**

Billy the Squid.

**Have you heard the joke
about the peach?**

It's pitiful.

**Which bird can hold three gallons
of water in its bill?**

The pelican.

**Where does Spider-Man go for
medical advice?**

Web MD.

Q&A

Why was the potato alone at the party?

It got there oily.

What's the best time to visit the dentist?

Tooth-hurty!

Which state needs a handkerchief?

Mass-ACHOO!-setts.

Why do fish choirs always sing off-key?

Because you can't tuna fish.

What kind of undies do clouds wear?

Thunderwear!

Q&A

**Did you hear about the frog
that was illegally parked?**

It got toad.

**Why did the toilet paper
roll down the hill?**

To get to the bottom.

**If April showers bring May flowers,
what do May flowers bring?**

Pilgrims!

**What do you call a motorcycle with a
good sense of humor?**

A Yamahahaha.

Why did the kid leave his piggy bank outside?

He expected some change in the weather.

Why didn't the teddy bear eat his oatmeal?

He was already stuffed!

What kind of books do skunks read?

Best-smellers.

Why do vampires brush their teeth?

To prevent bat breath.

Q&A

**Where do baby ghosts
spend their days?**

At day-scare centers.

What do you call a sleeping T. rex?

A dino-snore!

**Why did the cantaloupe jump
into the lake?**

It wanted to be a watermelon.

Why did the belt get arrested?

It held up a pair of pants.

Why are batteries always sad?

Because they're never included.

How can you fall off a 100-foot ladder without getting hurt?

Easy! Fall from the bottom rung.

How is Facebook like a refrigerator?

Because every few minutes you open it to see if there's anything good in it.

If Pilgrims were alive today, what would they be most famous for?

Their age!

Q&A

**What's the best day to go
to the beach?**

Sun-day.

**What do baby sweet potatoes
wear to bed?**

Their yammies!

**What's green, has big eyes, and is
hard to see through?**

Kermit the Fog.

What kind of car does a farmer drive?

A corn-vertible.

**Where do you send a shoe
in the summer?**

Boot camp!

**Why were the early days of history
called the Dark Ages?**

Because there were so many knights.

**What did one car muffler say to the
other car muffler?**

"Boy, am I exhausted!"

**What should you shout if you swim into
kelp and get caught in it?**

"Kelp!"

Q&A

What lives at the bottom of the ocean and is popular on Easter?

Oyster eggs.

What do you say to a hitchhiking angel?

"Harp in!"

How do you make antifreeze?

Steal her blanket.

What has a big mouth but can't talk?

A jar.

What's red and smells like blue paint?

Red paint.

2

DOGS & CATS

Which kind of dog can jump higher than a building?

Any dog. Buildings can't jump.

What looks like half of a cat?

The other half.

22

**What do cats like to eat
for dessert?**

Mice cream.

**What should you know before
you teach a dog a trick?**

More than the dog!

Which movie is a feline favorite?

The Sound of Mew-sic.

**Why can dogs scratch whenever
they want to?**

They live in a flea country.

What did the alien say to the cat?

"Take me to your litter!"

Will: If you want to find your dog, you should put an ad in the paper.

Bill: Don't be silly. Fido can't read!

Which cats make the best bowlers?

Alley cats.

Why are dogs such terrible dancers?

They have two left feet.

How do you spell mousetrap using three letters? C-A-T!

DOGS & CATS

What did the dog say when it sat on the sandpaper?

Ruff.

Cat: What smells the most in a garbage dump?

Rat: The nose.

Which household cleaner do dalmatians fear most?

Spot remover.

What do you call a guy who's been attacked by a cat?

Claude!

Why did the dog say "Meow"?

He was trying to learn
a second language.

What's a cat's favorite song?

"Three Blind Mice."

**What do you get when you cross
a dog and a dandelion?**

A collie-flower.

**Which game do cats like to
play with mice?**

Catch!

Where do dogs go when their tails fall off?

The retail store.

How do cats end a fight?

They hiss and make up.

What did the dalmatian say after eating?

"That hit the spots!"

What's smarter than a talking cat?

A spelling bee.

## DOGS & CATS

**How do fleas get from one dog
to another dog?**

By itch-hiking.

**Why was the kitten in such a
bad mood?**

She needed a catnap.

Why did the dog cross the road...twice?

To fetch a boomerang!

What do cats like to put in their milk?

Mice cubes.

Which breed of dog loves taking baths?

Shampoodles!

Why do cats scratch themselves?

Because no one else knows
where the itch is.

How do you keep a dog from smelling?

Put a clothespin on its nose.

Why can't cats finish watching DVDs?

They can't resist pressing
the "paws" button.

What did one flea say to the other flea when they walked out of the movie?

"Shall we walk or take the dog?"

What do you call a giant pile of cats?

A meowtain.

What do sheepdogs turn into every summer?

Hot dogs!

Why are cats terrible storytellers?

They only have one tail.

DOGS & CATS

Why do dogs run around in circles?

It's hard to run around in squares.

What breakfast cereal do cats like best?

Mice Krispies!

Why did the Dachshund bite his trainer's ankle?

He couldn't reach any higher.

What do you call a cat that just swallowed a duck?

A duck-filled fatty puss.

When is a bloodhound dumb?

When it has no scents.

Why do cats climb trees?

Because they don't have ladders.

Why did the terrier have splinters in his tongue?

He kept eating table scraps.

When is it bad luck to have a black cat cross your path?

When you're a mouse!

Which holiday do dogs like best?

Howl-o-ween.

What do you get if you cross a rabbit with two cats?

Hare! Kitty kitty!

Which dogs make the best teachers?

Grade Danes.

How can you tell if a cat burglar has been in your house?

Your cat is missing.

3

YUM YUKS!

What does Godzilla eat at a restaurant?

The restaurant!

Why couldn't the bagel escape?

It was covered with lox.

YUM YUKS!

What kind of candy do you eat on the playground?

Recess Pieces.

Why did the beet turn red?

It saw the salad dressing.

Did you hear about the crazy pancake?

He just flipped!

What is Peter Pan's favorite fast-food restaurant?

Wendy's.

Who makes shoes for fruit?

A peach cobbler.

How do you fix a broken pizza?

With tomato paste.

Who writes nursery rhymes and squeezes oranges?

Mother Juice.

Kid: Waiter! There's a bee in my soup.

Waiter: Of course. You ordered alphabet soup.

What was the snowman's favorite cereal?

Frosted Flakes.

Which food can you eat in the bathroom?

Showerkraut.

What's green, has 22 legs, and plays football?

The Green Bay Pickles.

Why did the pie go to the dentist?

It needed a filling.

What's brown, wrinkled, and lives in a tower?

The Lunch Bag of Notre Dame.

What do you get when you cross a pig and a centipede?

Bacon and legs.

Why did the baker stop making doughnuts?

He was tired of the hole business.

Did you hear about the guy who drank food coloring?

He dyed a little inside.

YUM YUKS!

What starts with a T, ends with a T,
and is full of T?

A teapot.

What does the ocean eat for breakfast?

Boatmeal.

Why are tightrope walkers so healthy?

They always eat a balanced diet.

What do computers snack on?

Microchips.

What do you call a baby potato?

A small fry.

YUM YUKS!

**What did the baby corn say to
the mama corn?**

"Where's Popcorn?"

Why did the cookie visit the doctor?

It was feeling crummy.

**What do you call a potato at
a football game?**

A spec-tater!

**What was the anteater's
favorite pizza topping?**

Antchovies!

**What do you get when you cross a bee
with chopped meat?**

Humburger.

**What did the banana do when it saw a
horde of hungry monkeys?**

Split.

**Why did the kid stare at frozen
orange juice can all day?**

Because the label said "concentrate."

What does a nosy pepper do?

Gets jalapeño business.

A kid walks into a soda shop with a slab of asphalt under his arm and says, "A root beer please, and one for the road."

Which potato makes the best detective?

One whose eyes are peeled.

What did the hot dog say when it won the race?

"I'm a weiner!"

What happens when the chef goes on strike?

You have a cook-out.

YUM YUKS!

What does a panda fry his bamboo in?

A pan...duh!

What did the frog order at McDonald's?

Flies and a diet croak.

Dad: Sorry, son, but I only know how to make two dishes, meat loaf and apple pie.

Son: Which one is this?

Why did the potato cross the road?

It saw a fork up ahead.

Best Cookbook: *Hot Dog* by Frank Furter

YUM YUKS!

**What did one plate say to
the other plate?**

"Lunch is on me!"

What kind of nut doesn't have a shell?

A doughnut.

**Did you hear the joke about the
pepperoni pizza?**

Never mind. It's way too cheesy.

**What kind of ice cream is
bad at tennis?**

Soft serve.

YUM YUKS!

Which day do eggs hate?

Fry-day.

Which food stays hot in the fridge?

Hot dogs.

What do ghosts eat for lunch?

Boo-loney sandwiches.

What do you call a stolen yam?

A hot potato.

What do you call a small hot dog?

A teenie weenie!

How do you make soup into gold?

Add 14 carrots.

What does a snowman put in his coffee?

Cold cream.

Why was the salad naked?

The waitress forgot the dressing.

Why don't tomatoes like to box?

They get beat to a pulp.

What is a tree's favorite drink?

Root beer.

YUM YUKS!

When does hot chocolate cause a stabbing pain in the eye?

When you forget to take out the spoon!

Where does Santa go to buy potatoes?

Idaho-ho-ho!

Why did the kid have string beans stuck up his nose?

He wasn't eating properly.

It was so hot...

...the cornfield popped,

...the cows gave evaporated milk,

...the grapes turned to raisins, and

...the chickens laid hard-boiled eggs!

4

What do you call a stupid pirate?

The pillage idiot.

Why couldn't the pirate play cards?

He was sitting on the deck!

ARRR!

Why did the pirate walk the plank?

Because he couldn't afford a dog.

Which pirate makes the best clam chowder?

Captain Cook!

Why did the pirate put a chicken on top of his treasure chest?

Because eggs mark the spot.

What did the pirate say when his wooden leg got stuck in a snowbank?

"Shiver me timbers!"

Why wouldn't the pirate fight
the octopus?

It was too well-armed.

What type of socks do pirates wear?

Arrrrrgyle.

Why did the pirate buy an eye patch?

He couldn't afford an iPhone.

Why didn't the pirate take a bath
before he walked the plank?

He knew he would just wash up on
shore later.

ARRR!

What did the pirate say on his 80th birthday?

"Aye, matey!"

Where do pirate ships go when they're sick?

To the dock.

Where can you find a pirate who has lost his wooden legs?

Right where you left him.

What's a pirate's favorite vegetable?

Arrrrrtichoke.

ARRR!

First Mate: Feeding the prisoners to the sharks isn't any fun.

Captain: It is for the sharks!

What happened when the red pirate ship sank in the Black Sea?

The crew was marooned.

Why are pirates called pirates?

Because they just arrrrr!

Why do pirate captains always sing tenor?

They're the only ones who can hit the high Cs.

Where did the pirate leave his keys?

Off the coast of Florida.

What do you call a pirate with two eyes and two legs?

Rookie.

What has eight arms, eight legs, and eight eyes?

Eight pirates.

Where did the one-legged pirate go for breakfast?

IHOP.

**What is the pirate's favorite
letter in the alphabet?**

X...That's where the treasure is.

**How much do pirates pay
for their earrings?**

A buck an ear (buccaneer).

**Did you hear about the new *Pirates of
the Caribbean* movie?**

It was rated Arrr!

Why was it rated Arrr?

Too much booty!

ARRR!

What do you call a pirate droid?

Arrr2-D2

What happened to the pirate who couldn't pee?

He became arrrate (irate).

What's the difference between a jeweler and the captain of a ship?

One sees the watches and the other watches the seas.

How does a pirate know when the sea is friendly?

It waves.

5

FAIRY FUNNY!

Who helped Fisherella get to the ball?

Her fairy codmother.

Why did Robin Hood steal money from the rich?

Because the poor didn't have any.

FAIRY FUNNY!

Who was the fattest knight at King Arthur's Round Table?

Sir Cumference.

What do you call a princess who falls down on the ice?

Slipping Beauty.

On which side of the house did Jack grow the beanstalk?

The outside.

Why is Tinker Bell always flying around?

Because she lives in Neverland.

FAIRY FUNNY!

Why did Cinderella get kicked off the soccer team?

She kept running away from the ball.

First Dragon: Am I too late for dinner?

Second Dragon: Yes. Everyone's eaten.

Who weighs two tons and went to the ball wearing glass slippers?

Cinderelephant.

Why did Robin Hood's men hate living in Sherwood Forest?

It only had one Little John.

FAIRY FUNNY!

Who carves wooden figures and lives under the sea?

The Whittle Mermaid.

What do you get if you cross Tinker Bell with a werewolf?

A hairy fairy.

What do you get if you cross a hairy fairy with a monster?

A scary hairy fairy.

What laundry detergent does the Little Mermaid use?

Tide.

FAIRY FUNNY!

Optician: Have your eyes ever been checked?

Ogre: No. They've always been red.

Why does Snow White treat all of the dwarves equally?

Because she's the fairest of them all.

How did Jack know how many beans his cow was worth?

He used a cowculator.

Fairyland Best-sellers:

How to Cook Crocodile by Stu Potts

Aladdin's Lamp: The Inside Story by A. Genie

Who Killed Captain Hook? by Howard I. Know

FAIRY FUNNY!

Why can't Goldilocks sleep?

Night-bears!

Why did the Little Mermaid blush?

She saw the ship's bottom!

Why did Rapunzel go to parties?

She liked to let her hair down!

How is Prince Charming like a book?

He has a lot of pages.

What do you call a wee cottage?

A gnome home.

FAIRY FUNNY!

What is Humpty Dumpty's least favorite season?

Fall.

Who stole the soap from the Three Bears' bathroom?

The robber ducky.

What did Peter Pan say when he saw the tornado?

"Look! It's Wendy."

Why didn't the Fairy Godmother laugh at Cinderella's jokes?

They weren't fairy funny.

FAIRY FUNNY!

Where does Robin Hood like to shop?

At Target.

Who's the smartest fairy in Neverland?

Thinker Bell.

What do you call a fairy that won't bathe?

Stinker Bell.

Why is the ocean floor so sandy?

There are never enough mermaids.

Why is the Tooth Fairy so smart?

She's collected a lot of wisdom teeth.

6

Knock-knock!

Who's there?

Comma.

Comma who?

Comma little closer and I'll tell you!

KNOCK-KNOCK!

Knock-knock!

Who's there?

Interrupting chicken.

Interrupting chick—

HEY! WANNA CROSS THE ROAD?

Knock-knock!

Who's there?

Dishes.

Dishes who?

Dishes the way I talk since I lost
my two front teeth!

Knock-knock!

Who's there?

Ya.

Ya who?

Sorry. I prefer Google.

KNOCK-KNOCK!

Knock-knock!
Who's there?
Amos.
Amos who?
A mosquito bit me.

Knock-knock!
Who's there?
Andy.
Andy who?
Andy bit me again!

Knock-knock!
Who's there?
Omelette.
Omelette who?
Omelette smarter than I look.

KNOCK-KNOCK!

Why did the duck cross the road?

To get to your house.

Knock-knock!

Who's there?

The duck!

Knock-knock!

Who's there?

Stan.

Stan who?

Stan back! I'm going to kick the door down.

M-O-O...!

Knock-knock!

Who's there?

Time-traveling cow.

Knock-knock!
Who's there?
Deluxe.
Deluxe who?
Deluxe-smith. I'm here to fix de lock.

Knock-knock!
Who's there?
Ida.
Ida who?
Ida called first but my cell phone died.

Knock-knock!
Who's there?
Howdy!
Howdy who?
Howdy do that?

KNOCK-KNOCK!

Knock-knock!
Who's there?
Euripides.
Euripides who?
Euripides pants you buy me new ones.

Knock-knock!
Who's there?
Cows go.
Cows go who?
No, silly! Cows go "MOO"!

Knock-knock!
Who's there?
Interrupting zombie.
Interrupting zom—
"BRAAAINS!"

KNOCK-KNOCK!

Knock-knock!
Who's there?
Europe.
Europe who?
What? No, you're a poo!

Knock-knock!
Who's there?
Althea.
Althea who?
Althea later alligator!

Knock-knock!
Who's there?
Dare.
Dare who?
Dare must be some mistake!

KNOCK-KNOCK!

Knock-knock!
Who's there?
Dozen.
Dozen who?
Dozen anyone care that I'm stuck outside in the cold?

Knock-knock!
Who's there?
Topeka.
Topeka who?
Why do you like Topeka your nose?

Knock-knock!
Who's there?
Pig.
Pig who?
Pig me up after school, please!

KNOCK-KNOCK!

Knock-knock!
Who's there?
Kenya.
Kenya who?
Kenya come out and play after dinner?

Knock-knock!
Who's there?
Will Hugh.
Will Hugh who?
Will Hugh toss that ball back over the fence?

Knock-knock!
Who's there?
Zeeno.
Zeeno who?
Zeeno evil. Hear no evil.

KNOCK-KNOCK!

Knock-knock!
Who's there?
My panther.
My panther who?
My panther falling down.

Knock-knock!
Who's there?
Ooze.
Ooze who?
Ooze afraid of the Big Bad Wolf?

Knock-knock!
Who's there?
Weird.
Weird who?
Weird you hide the chocolate?

KNOCK-KNOCK!

Knock-knock!
Who's there?
Yoda.
Yoda who?
Yoda weirdest person I know.

Knock-knock!
Who's there?
Skip.
Skip who?
Just skip it. I'll go next door.

Knock-knock!
Who's there?
Tubby.
Tubby who?
Tubby or not Tubby?
That is the question.

KNOCK-KNOCK!

Knock-knock!
Who's there?
I am.
I am who?
You mean you don't know?

Knock-knock!
Who's there?
Wooden.
Wooden who?
Wooden you like to know!

Knock-knock!
Who's there?
Saul.
Saul who?
Saul there is, there ain't no more!

7

Why do elephants wear tennies?

Because ninies are too small and elevenies are too big!

What is big and gray and blue?

An elephant holding its breath.

ELEPHANTS

**Why did the elephant
change his socks?**

Because they were dirty.

Why do elephants have a trunk?

They would look silly carrying a hatbox.

**What did the worm say after he crawled
under the elephant's foot?**

I'll never have the guts to
do that again!

**What's worse than an elephant with
no shirt on?**

A hippo-bottomless.

What time is it when an elephant sits on the fence?

Time to get a new fence.

What time is it when an elephant sits on an electric fence?

Time to get a new elephant!

Why do elephants paint their toenails red, yellow, orange, green, and brown?

So they can hide in a bag of M&Ms.

Why didn't the elephant wear pajamas at camp?

He forgot to pack his trunk.

Why do ducks have webbed feet?

To stamp out forest fires.

Where do elephants with zits go?

To the pachydermatologist.

Why do elephants have flat feet?

To stamp out flaming ducks!

Which elephants live in the Arctic?

The cold ones.

What's big, gray, and lives in Scotland?

The Loch Ness Elephant.

ELEPHANTS

What kind of elephants live at the North Pole?

Elfaphants.

What do you get when you cross an elephant with peanut butter?

An elephant that sticks to the roof of your mouth.

Why are elephants large, gray, and wrinkled?

If they were small, round, and white, they'd be aspirins.

Why can't you take an elephant to school?

It won't fit in your backpack.

How do you tell an elephant from a dozen eggs?

If you don't know, I'll send someone else to the store.

Why do elephants walk sideways through grass?

To trip the field mice.

What's gray and has four legs and a trunk?

A mouse going on vacation.

How do you get down from an elephant?

You don't. You get down from a duck.

What do you call an elephant that doesn't matter?

An irrelephant.

What goes *thump, thump, thump, squish*?

An elephant with one wet sneaker.

What do you get if you drop an elephant on a baby butterfly?

A splatterpillar.

How can you tell when there are three elephants in the bathtub with you?

You count them!

ELEPHANTS

What do you call an elephant that
never takes a bath?

A smellyphant.

Why did the elephant paint his toenails
different colors?

To hide in the jelly bean jar.

Have you ever found an elephant in
a jelly bean jar?

See? It works.

Who started the elephant jokes?

That's what the elephants
want to know.

ELEPHANTS

When does a baby elephant look like a cute little bunny?

When she's wearing a cute little bunny suit.

What do you do with old bowling balls?

Give them to elephants to use as marbles.

Why do elephants wear sandals?

So they don't sink in the sand.

Why do ostriches stick their head in the sand?

To look for the elephants who forgot to wear their sandals.

ELEPHANTS

Why do elephants have big ears?

To keep their sunglasses from
falling off.

Why do elephants wear sunglasses?

So Tarzan doesn't recognize them.

**What did Tarzan say when he
saw a herd of elephants running
through the jungle?**

Nothing. He didn't recognize them with
their sunglasses on.

**Why do elephants have
wrinkled knees?**

They tie their tennis shoes too tight.

8

HUMDINGERS

What did the drummer get on his IQ test?

Saliva.

Who is the wasp's favorite composer?

Bee-thoven.

HUMDINGERS

Did you hear about the cobra that hid in the tuba?

He was a real snake in the brass.

What has lots of keys but can't open doors?

A piano.

Why do bagpipers march when they play?

To get away from the noise.

Why did the rock star bring a pencil on stage?

He wanted to draw a big crowd.

What's the difference between an accordion and an onion?

No one cries when you chop up an accordion.

Did you hear about the band called 1023 Megabytes?

They were on their way to a gig.

What is the squirrel's favorite opera?

The Nutcracker.

What is the rabbit's favorite music?

Hip-hop!

HUMDINGERS

What's Beethoven's favorite fruit?

Ba-na-na-na!!!

What song do vampires hate?

"You Are My Sunshine."

Why did the pop star get arrested?

She got in treble!

What do you call a musical pickle?

A piccolo.

What's big and gray with horns?

An elephant marching band.

Why did the school band have such bad manners?

It didn't know how to conduct itself.

Why are pop stars so cool?

They have millions of fans.

Why did Mozart hate chickens?

They're always running around going "Bach! Bach! Bach!"

How do you get your dad to drive really fast?

Put your drums in the middle of the road.

Why did the chicken cross the road?

To get away from the oboe recital.

How do you clean a tuba?

With a tuba toothpaste.

Why don't guitarists work?

They only know how to play.

Why did the punk rocker cross the road?

He was stapled to a chicken.

Why was the guitar mad?

It was tired of being picked on.

HUMDINGERS

What kind of paper makes music?

Rapping paper!

Why did the pianist bang the side of his head against the keyboard?

He was playing by ear.

Where do vampire violinists go for vacation?

The Vile Inn.

What's the most musical part of a turkey?

The drumstick.

HUMDINGERS

What was stolen from the music store?

The lute!

How do you make a bandstand?

Take away their chairs!

Why do hummingbirds hum?

They forgot the words.

Why shouldn't kids go to the symphony?

Too much sax and violins.

What kind of band doesn't play music?

A rubber band.

9

When does the moon stop eating?

When it's full.

**What tastes better, a comet
or an asteroid?**

An asteroid, because it's meteor!

Why does E.T. have such big eyes?

He saw his phone bill.

**Which astronaut wears
the biggest helmet?**

The one with the biggest head.

How do you serve aliens dinner?

On flying saucers.

**Favorite Space Book:
Full Moon by Seymour Buns**

**How do astronauts keep warm on the
International Space Station?**

They turn up the space heater.

How do meteors stay clean?

They shower!

What does an astronaut wear to bed?

Space jammies.

What did the astronomer see at the center of Jupiter?

The letter i.

What's the difference between E.T. and a teenager?

E.T. actually phoned home.

Why did the space restaurant close down?

It lacked atmosphere.

What do you get when you cross a kangaroo with an alien?

A Mars-upial.

Did you hear about the astronaut who broke the law of gravity?

She got a suspended sentence.

Why was the moon acting so loony?

It was going through a phase.

**How does the universe
hold up its pants?**

With an asteroid belt.

**What do stars do when they
want a snack?**

Take a bite out of the Milky Way.

**How do you throw the best party in
the solar system?**

You planet.

What did the astronaut cook for lunch?

An unidentified frying object.

How do you get an astronaut's baby to fall asleep?

You rocket.

What is Han Solo's favorite restaurant?

Jabba the Pizza Hutt.

Captain Kirk: "Our next mission takes us to the Sun."

Scotty: "We canna do it, Captain! The sun is far too hot."

Captain Kirk: "Don't worry, Scotty. We'll land at night."

What kind of songs do astronauts like?

Neptunes!

What do you call a UFO with a leak?

A crying saucer.

What did the alien say to the garden?

Take me to your weeder.

How do Martians count to 13?

On their fingers.

Teacher: Which is closer, China or the moon?

Kid: Duh...the moon. You can't see China from here.

What was the alien's favorite taco filling?

Human beans.

SPACE CASE

Why did the chicken cross the galaxy?

To boldly go where no chicken
had gone before.

**Kid 1: I hear Dracula will be starring
in the next *Star Wars* movie.**

Kid 2: Really? What's it called?

Kid 1: *The Vampire Strikes Back.*

**What did the ones say to the twos
and threes?**

"May the fours be with you!"

What kind of life was found on Pluto?

Fleas.

When can't you visit the moon?

When it's full.

On which planet did the space probe crash?

Splaturn!

What do you get when you cross a toad with the sun?

Star warts.

Where do otters come from?

Otter space.

An astronaut's favorite fish: stardines.

SPACE CASE

What did E.T.'s mom say when he returned home?

"Where on Earth have you been?"

Why don't Martians drown in hot chocolate?

They sit on the Mars-mallows.

How does the moon cut his hair when the sun gets in the way?

Eclipse it.

Why did the space shuttle pilot eat beans every day?

He didn't want to run out of gas.

10

ONE-LINERS

Whatever you do, always give 100%.
Unless you're donating blood.

A kid goes to the store to buy some
toilet paper. The clerk asks him what
color he'd like. "White," says the kid.
"I'll color it myself!"

My friend told me an onion is the only food that makes you cry, so I threw a coconut at his face.

There's only one good thing about getting hit in the head with a can of Coke. It's a soft drink.

A pessimist's bloodtype is always B-negative.

Whoever invented knock-knock jokes should get a no-bell prize.

A magician was walking down the street and turned into a grocery store.

The time traveler was still hungry after his last bite, so he went back four seconds.

What is the difference between ignorance and apathy? I don't know, and I don't care.

A cowboy, a clown, and a fireman walk into a bar. Ow!

I was addicted to the hokey pokey... but I turned myself around. Isn't that what it's all about?

The wig thief struck again last night. Police are combing the area.

ONE-LINERS

Jokes about German sausages
are the wurst.

When fish are in schools, they
sometimes take debate.

A dog gave birth to puppies in the park
and was cited for littering.

Two silkworms had a race.
They ended up in a tie.

My dog can do magic tricks. It's a
labracadabrador.

I was struggling to figure out how
lightning works, then it struck me.

Parallel lines have so much in common.
It's a shame they'll never meet.

If Iron Man and the Silver Surfer
teamed up, they would be alloys.

Just went to an emotional wedding...
even the cake was in tiers.

Two antennae decided to get married.
The ceremony was dull, but the
reception was great!

Living on Earth might be expensive,
but at least you get a free trip
around the sun every year.

I know a lot of jokes about unemployed people, but none of them work.

Why do we cook bacon and bake cookies?

A black hole is a tunnel at the end of the light.

Time flies...when you throw your alarm clock across the room.

A rancher had 196 cows in his field, but when he rounded them up he had 200.

Taller kids always sleep longer.

I was up all night wondering where the sun had gone...then it dawned on me.

I would go rock climbing if I were a little boulder.

I used to have a fear of hurdles, but I got over it.

If a boomerang always comes back to you, why throw it in the first place?

Dad gave me a bat for my birthday, but the first time I tried to play with it, it flew away.

Dry-erase boards are remarkable.

Just wrote a song about a tortilla.
Actually, it was more of a wrap.

**Always keep a smile on your face. It
looks silly anywhere else on your body.**

Silence is golden. Duct tape is silver.

**Two wrongs don't make a right...but
two Wrights did make an airplane!**

To the guy who invented zero:
Thanks for nothing!

11

ANIMAL ANTICS

What kind of key opens a banana?

A monkey.

What did the pig say on the hottest day of summer?

"I'm bacon!"

ANIMAL ANTICS

Why do seagulls fly over the sea?

Because if they flew over the bay,
they'd be bagels.

What do you do with a blue whale?

Cheer it up!

What do you call a pig who knows karate?

Pork chop.

What do cows read in the morning?

Moospapers.

What clucks and points north?

A magnetic chicken.

ANIMAL ANTICS

What do you call a flying skunk?

A smelly-copter.

What do you call a sheep with no legs?

A cloud.

Why were the owl parents worried about their son?

Because he didn't seem to give a hoot about anything.

What's the difference between a cow and a doughnut?

It's a lot harder to dunk a cow in a cup of coffee.

ANIMAL ANTICS

Why did the cow jump over the moon?

The farmer had cold hands.

Why are frogs so happy?

They eat what bugs them.

What's the strongest bird?

The crane.

What has six eyes but can't see?

Three blind mice.

What do you call a sleeping bull?

A bulldozer.

ANIMAL ANTICS

How does a pig get to the hospital?

In a hambulance.

What does a spider bride wear?

A webbing dress.

Why did the canary fail his test?

He was caught tweeting.

Why was the little ant so confused?

Because all of his uncles were ants.

Why did the rhino wear red sneakers?

Because the blue ones were dirty.

ANIMAL ANTICS

Why do seals prefer swimming in salt water?

Because pepper water makes them sneeze.

Where do cows go for first dates?

To the moo-vies.

What's orange, has stripes, and is red all over?

A tiger with a sunburn.

What do you get if you cross a parrot with a shark?

A bird that will talk your ear off.

ANIMAL ANTICS

How is a turtle like a brick?

Neither one can play the trumpet.

How do you make a milk shake?

Give a cow a pogo stick.

Why do turkeys gobble?

They never learned table manners.

Why do skunks like Valentine's Day?

They're very scent-imental.

How do ducklings escape their shells?

They eggs-it.

ANIMAL ANTICS

Why did the chicken cross the road?

The light was green.

**Why did the bubble gum
cross the road?**

Because it was stuck to
the chicken's foot.

**What looks like a snake, swims,
and honks?**

An automob-eel.

**Why couldn't the leopard escape
from the zoo?**

He was always spotted.

What do you get if you cross a canary with a 20-foot snake?

A sing-a-long.

Why don't you ever see hippos hiding in trees?

Because they're very good at it.

What did the chicken say when it laid a square egg?

Ouch!

What do you call a bear with no teeth?

A gummy bear.

What's the difference between bird flu and swine flu?

For bird flu, you need tweetment.
For swine flu, you need oinkment.

What do you call a man with 50 rabbits under his coat?

Warren.

What do you get when you cross a cow and a duck?

Milk and quackers.

What's a firefly's life motto?

Always look on the bright side.

ANIMAL ANTICS

What do you call a dinosaur wearing high heels?

A My-feet-are-saurus.

Which dinosaur had the biggest vocabulary?

Thesaurus.

What do you call a paranoid dinosaur?

A Do-you-think-he-saurus?

How do you dress for a dinosaur party?

In a suit of armor.

ANIMAL ANTICS

Why don't dinosaurs talk?

Because they're all dead!

What's the biggest moth in the world?

A mammoth.

How can you tell if a dinosaur is a plant-eater or a meat-eater?

Lie down on a plate and see what happens.

Why was T. rex afraid to visit the library?

His books were 60 million years overdue.

What do you call the dumbest fish
in school?

Dinner.

Why did the marsupial from Australia
get fired from his job?

Because he wasn't koala-fied.

Why did the cowboy buy a dachshund?

Because someone told him to get a
long little doggy.

Why did the cow cross the road?

To get to the udder side.

ANIMAL ANTICS

How do you keep geese from speeding?

Goose bumps.

What did the buffalo say to his son when he left for school?

"Bison!"

What kind of monkey likes potato chips?

A chipmunk.

What do you call a sheep covered in chocolate?

A candy baa.

What do you call a girl with a frog on her head?

Lily.

Why shouldn't you play poker in the savanna?

Too many cheetahs.

What's black and white, black and white, and black and white?

A panda rolling down a hill.

What do you call a sheep that dances gracefully?

A baaaaaalerina.

ANIMAL ANTICS

What do you call a cow with four legs?

A cow.

How do pigs communicate with each other?

Swine language.

How do ants keep warm in the winter?

Ant-ifreeze.

What do you call a fly with no wings?

A walk!

Who's a boar's favorite painter?

Pig-casso.

What's big, gray, and wrinkly, and goes around in circles?

A rhinoceros in a revolving door.

What do frogs wear in the summer?

Open toad shoes.

Why do pigs have the best writing instruments?

Because their pens never run out of oink.

Why did the chicken cross the schoolyard?

To get to the other slide!

12

'SNOT FUNNY

When is a booger not a booger?

When it's snot.

Which nut catches the most colds?

The cashew.

'SNOT FUNNY

What can you tie boogers into?

A snot.

Where does your nose go when it gets hungry?

Booger King.

What is the difference between a booger and a plate?

The plate goes ON the table.
The booger goes UNDER the table.

What do boogers and apples have in common?

They both get picked and eaten.

What's the difference between boogers and brussels sprouts?

Kids won't eat brussels sprouts.

What did the booger say when the team captains were choosing players?

"Pick me! Pick me!"

What do you find in a clean nose?

Fingerprints!

What happens when you sneeze without using a tissue?

You take matters into your own hands.

'SNOT FUNNY

Why do elephants have long fingernails?

So they can pick their trunks.

Who was hiding under little Sammy's bed?

The boogie man.

Which king plays a bagpipe, wears a kilt, and sneezes all the time?

The King of Snotland.

What did the booger say to his girlfriend?

"I'm stuck on you."

'SNOT FUNNY

What's green and hangs from a tree?

Giraffe snot.

Why do farmers have noses?

So they have something to pick while they wait for their crops to grow.

Why didn't the nose make the volleyball team?

Nobody picked him.

Why shouldn't you eat boogers?

Because you don't want to spoil your dinner.

'SNOT FUNNY

Why is a haunted handkerchief scary?

Because it's covered in boo-gers.

Why don't dinosaurs pick their noses?

Because they don't want to eat 20-pound boogers.

Why was the snowman looking for carrots at the grocery store?

He wanted to pick his nose.

What runs in big families?

The same thing that runs in small families: noses.

How do you make a tissue dance?

Put a little boogy in it!

What did one booger say to the other?

"You think you're funny but you're snot."

What's gross?

Finding a hair in your food.

What's grosser than gross?

Finding out it's your grandma's nose hair.

Why do gorillas have large nostrils?

Because they have fat fingers.

'SNOT FUNNY

When is a fence like a nose?

When it's a picket fence.

What did the big booger say to
the little booger?

"Don't get snotty with me!"

Knock-knock!
Who's there?
Adam's not.
Adam's not who?
Adam's not is dripping from his nose.

What do you call a booger that's
wearing a helmet?

A snail.

'SNOT FUNNY

What do you do if your nose
goes on strike?

Picket.

Why did the booger cross the road?

Because he was being picked on.

Why do farmers have noses?

So they'll have something to pick
in the winter.

What happened when the elephant
sat on a quarter?

A booger popped out of George
Washington's nose.

'SNOT FUNNY

**What's yellow and gooey
and smells like bananas?**

Monkey snot.

Why was the nose sad?

It didn't get picked.

Knock-knock!
Who's there?
Decode.
Decode who?
Decode in my nose is getting worse.

What's in a ghost's nose?

Boo-gers.

13

WHO FARTED?

Did you hear the joke about the fart?

It stinks.

What's the smelliest UFO?

An Unidentified Farting Object.

WHO FARTED?

Sam and Janet are taking a walk when Sam lets out a huge fart.

"Ugh," says Janet, "please stop it!"

"I would," replies Sam, "but I don't know which way it went."

How do you tell one end of a worm from the other?

Put it in a bowl of flour and wait for it to fart.

Who wears a red cape and farts in the forest?

Little Rude Riding Hood.

How does a ghost fart?

Out of its boo-ty.

141

WHO FARTED?

What do you get if you fart on your birthday?

A birthday farty.

What happened when the kid held his breath to stop himself from burping?

He farted.

Why did the taxi driver fart?

Because his cab ran out of gas.

How is a ninja like a fart?

They're both silent but deadly.

WHO FARTED?

Which Egyptian ruler farted a lot?

King Tootincoming.

What's invisible and smells like carrots?

Bunny farts!

What did the skunk say when the wind changed directions?

"It's all coming back to me now!"

How are rainbows made?

When unicorns fart.

WHO FARTED?

Why should you only put 239 beans in bean soup?

One more would make it too farty (240).

Why did the skeleton burp?

Because it didn't have the guts to fart.

What do you call a king's fart?

Noble gas.

What place should you avoid if you don't want to fart?

The gas station.

WHO FARTED?

What's the one thing a person won't do after they fart?

Admit it.

When does a boy take a bubble bath?

When he eats beans for dinner.

Why can't you smell alien farts?

Because they're out of this world.

What do you call a cat who likes to eat beans?

Puss 'n' Toots.

WHO FARTED?

Two flies sit on a pile of poop.
One fly passes gas.
The other fly looks at him and says,
"Hey, do you mind? I'm eating here."

What do you call someone who doesn't
fart in public?

A private tooter.

What do you get when you mix a
matchstick and a fart?

A flamethrower.

What hits the nose when aimed
at the feet?

A fart.

WHO FARTED?

Why don't bees fart?

Their stingers might fall off.

Knock-knock!
Who's there?
Gas.
Gas who?
Gas who just farted!

What is the sharpest thing in the world?

A fart. It goes through your pants and doesn't even leave a hole.

How are snowflakes made?

When snowmen fart.

WHO FARTED?

What do you call a professional farter?

A tutor.

What causes cold winter winds?

Frosty the Snowman eating beans.

What did the mouse say when he found his favorite cheese in cubes?

Who cut the cheese?

Did you hear about the man who went to jail for air pollution?

His farts were just that bad.

WHO FARTED?

How can you tell when a moth farts?

He flies straight for a second.

What happens when a clown farts?

It smells funny.

What happened when the kid ate baked beans before church?

He had to sit in his own pew.

What do you get when you mix beans and onions?

Tear gas.

WHO FARTED?

How is a filling station like a burrito?

They both supply you with gas.

What did the underwear say to the fart?

It's time for a change.

**Why should you never fart in
an Apple store?**

Because they don't have Windows.

**Why did little Johnny Gass
win the race?**

Because nobody wanted to pass Gass.

WHO FARTED?

How do you know when Grandpa's getting old?

When he farts, dust comes out.

Why did the fart get in trouble at the library?

Because he was too loud.

Where did Cinderella go to the bathroom?

In a land fart, fart away.

What's invisible and smells like bananas?

A monkey fart.

14

BR-A-A-AINS!

Why did the zombie eat the archer?

He wanted his bone and marrow.

Why did the zombie go to the dentist?

To improve his bite.

BR-A-A-AINS!

What is the zombie's favorite TV show?

Chomping on the Stars.

**Why did the little zombie stay home
from school?**

He was feeling rotten.

**Why didn't the zombie cross
the freeway?**

Because he didn't have the guts.

Where do zombies live?

On dead-end streets.

Zombie Kid: Mom, Why do you look so tired?

Mombie: Because I'm dead on my feet.

Why did the zombie cross the road?

To eat the chicken.

What's a zombie's favorite meal?

A Manwich.

What's black and white and dead all over?

A zombie in a tuxedo.

What kind of engagement ring did the zombie give his girlfriend?

A tombstone.

What did the zombie say when he saw his favorite movie star?

"I've been dying to eat you!"

When do zombies wake up?

At ate-o'clock.

Why did the zombie take a nap?

He was dead tired.

Why do zombies only date smart girls?

They just love a woman with
br-a-a-ains.

**When zombies break into a house,
where do they look for food?**

In the living room.

**What did the zombie say to the other
zombie who wanted to fight?**

"You wanna piece of me?"

**What kind of birds do zombies
like to eat the most?**

Cra-a-anes!

BR-A-A-AINS!

Why did the zombie sprinkle cheese powder on people's feet?

He wanted Doritoes.

Did you hear about the zombie hairdresser?

She dyed on the job.

Do dark circles around the eyes make a zombie look dead?

No, but being dead does.

What should you do if zombies surround your house?

Pray that it's Halloween.

BR-A-A-AINS!

What was the zombie kid's favorite game?

Corpse and robbers.

Why did the zombie eat the gym teacher?

He liked health food.

Why didn't the zombie finish eating the clown?

He tasted funny.

What did the zombie eat after its teeth were pulled?

The dentist.

BR-A-A-AINS!

What does a vegetarian zombie like to eat?

Gra-a-ains!

What did the zombie say to the locksmith?

"You're out of lock."

Which candy do zombie kids refuse?

Life Savers.

Why did the zombie eat a bowl of Cheerios?

He wanted to be a cereal killer.

BR-A-A-AINS!

Why did the zombie ignore his new Facebook friends?

He was busy digesting his old Facebook friends.

What do zombies like to eat at Christmastime?

Candy ca-a-anes!

What does a zombie order at a restaurant?

The waiter.

What did the zombie say to the watchmaker?

"Your time is up."

Zombie Kid: Mommy, do I have Daddy's eyes?

Mombie: Yes, dear. Now eat them before they get too cold.

What do you get when you cross a zombie with a snowman?

Frostbite.

How can you tell if a zombie is upset?

It falls to pieces.

What kind of bread do healthy zombies eat?

100 percent whole brain.

BR-A-A-AINS!

What's the zombie's favorite type of weather?

When it ra-a-a-ains!

How did the zombie ace the math test?

It was a no-brainer.

What does a zombie like to put on his br-a-a-ains?

Grave-y.

What's grosser than a dead zombie in the trash can?

A dead zombie in three thrash cans.

BR-A-A-AINS!

**Why did the rotting zombie
quit teaching?**

She only had one pupil.

What do you call an undead wasp?

A zom-bee.

**Do zombies eat popcorn
with their fingers?**

No, they eat the fingers separately.

Why did the zombie go crazy?

He had lost his mind.

15

REAL STINKERS

What do you call a vegetarian
with diarrhea?

A salad shooter.

Why did the superhero flush the toilet?

It was his duty.

Why can't you hear a pterodactyl going to the bathroom?

Because the "p" is silent.

What is brown and sticky?

A stick.

Knock-knock!
Who's there?
Butternut.
Butternut who?
Butternut step in the steaming pile of horse manure!

Who is the most constipated of all artists?

Vincent Can't Go.

Toothbrush: I hate my job.

Toilet paper: You think your job stinks? Try mine!

Why is pea soup more special than mashed potatoes?

Because anyone can mash potatoes.

What did the rooster say when he stepped in a cow pie?

"Cock-a-doodle-poo!"

What isn't an elephant a good pet?

It takes too long to clean the litter box.

REAL STINKERS

Who lives in the toilet and fights crime with ninja powers?

The Teenage Mutant Ninja Turdles.

What vegetables belong in a toilet?

Peas.

Knock-knock!
Who's there?
Enid.
Enid who?
Enid a clean pair of underwear NOW!

What's brown and sounds like a bell?

DUNGGGGGG!

Mother: Billy! Why are you sitting on the toilet and hitting yourself on the head?

Billy: Works for ketchup!

What do you call a part-time teacher who eats beans for lunch?

A substi-toot.

Why was the sand wet?

Because the sea weed.

What is big, green, and incredibly smelly?

The Hulk's farts!

Why did Captain Kirk go into the ladies' room?

He wanted to go where no man had gone before.

Your feet are so smelly, your shoes hid in the closet and refused to come out.

Knock-knock!
Who's there?
European.
European who?
European all over the floor!

Why couldn't the toilet paper cross the road?

It got stuck in a crack.

Student: May I go to the bathroom?

Teacher: Yes, but say your ABCs first.

Student: A B C D E F G H I J K L M N O Q R S T U V W X Y Z.

Teacher: Where is the P?

Student: Running down my leg.

Whaddaya call it when you go #1 before watching a movie?

A pee-quel.

Doctor: Four out of five people suffer from diarrhea.

Patient: Does that mean that one person enjoys it?

REAL STINKERS

What's dumb?

Directions on toilet paper.

What's dumber than that?

Reading them.

Even dumber than that?

Reading them and learning
something.

The dumbest of all?

Reading them and having to correct
something that you've been doing wrong.

If you're an American outside the bathroom, what are you inside the bathroom?

European!

What happens when babies eat Rice Krispies?

Snap, crackle, poop!

Did you hear the one about the elephant with diarrhea?

You should have, it's all over town.

What do you get if you cross a worm and a goat?

A dirty kid.

If there's H_2O on the inside of
a fire hydrant, what's on
the outside?

K9P.

How do website developers ask each
other where the bathroom is?

"Can you tell me the IP address?"

Why didn't anyone see the movie about
constipation?

It never came out.

What do you get when you cross a
dinosaur with a skunk?

A U-stink-asaurus.

Knock-knock!

Who's there?

Snow.

Snow who?

Snow fun to clean up elephant poop.

**What do flies and stinky feet
have in common?**

You can shoe them, but they
never go away.

**Why did the man bring a toilet to
the party?**

He was a party pooper.

**Your toenails are so long, you can cut
the grass by walking barefoot.**

What did the judge say when the skunk walked into the courtroom?

"Odor in the court!"

Thieves broke into the police station and stole all of the toilets. The police are investigating, but for now...they have nothing to go on.

What is the stinkiest dog?

The poo-dle.

Where did the rainbow go to the bathroom?

In the pot of gold.

**Why did Tigger stick his head
in the toilet?**

He was looking for Pooh.

**What do you call it when you step in
alien droppings?**

A close encounter of the turd kind.

Knock-knock!
Who's there?
Distinct.
Distinct who?
Distinct of skunk is awful!

**Flatulence: The emergency vehicle that
picks you up after you are run over
by a steamroller.**

Why did the roll of toilet paper quit its job?

It was pooped.

Farting on an elevator is wrong on so many levels.

Knock-knock!
Who's there?
Sabrina.
Sabrina who?
Sabrina long time since I changed my underwear!

What did the first mate see when he looked down the toilet?

The captain's log.

What do they say about a bird in the hand?

It can't poop on your head.

How do you keep flies out of the kitchen?

Put a big pile of manure in the living room.

Why did the fart cross the road?

It was trying to escape the stink.

Fart: A turd honking for the right of way.

Did you hear about Robin Hood's toilet?

He had a Little John.

What has two legs, one wheel, and stinks?

A wheelbarrow full of manure.

What's a volcano?

A mountain with the runs.

Where do bees go to the bathroom?

The BP station.

16

DON'T EAT THAT!

Why couldn't the snake talk?

He had a frog in his throat.

What do cats eat for breakfast?

Mice Krispies.

DON'T EAT THAT!

What's green, fuzzy, and sits in a bun?

A school lunch hamburger.

What's green, fuzzy, and sits on a toilet for hours?

The kid who ate the school lunch hamburger.

What's the difference between a worm and a blueberry?

Have you ever tried eating a worm pie?

How do you keep a loaf of bread warm all day?

Let a cat sleep on it.

DON'T EAT THAT!

What did the spider order at McDonald's?

French flies.

What do you call a worm in an apple?

Teacher's pet.

How do you make a maggot stew?

Keep the maggot waiting for a couple of hours.

What's the difference between school lunch and a pair of smelly socks?

In an emergency, you can eat the smelly socks.

Which cafeteria food makes you throw up?

Spew-ghetti.

Kid: Mommy! Mommy! What happened to the dry dog food Fido wouldn't eat?

Mom: Be quiet and eat your cereal.

What do you get when you cross a turkey with a centipede?

Drumsticks for everybody!

Why did the farmer eat his foot?

Because there was a corn on it.

DON'T EAT THAT!

What's a mushroom?

The place they store school lunches.

What's sticky, purple, has 16 legs, and is covered with thick, brown hair?

I don't know, but it's on your lunch tray.

How do you know that owls are smarter than chickens?

Have you ever eaten fried owl?

What do you get when you throw up Chef Boyardee canned pasta?

Barf-a-Roni.

DON'T EAT THAT!

Why didn't Batman go fishing?

Because Robin ate all the worms.

What's green, comes on a bun, and is covered in ketchup and mustard?

A hot frog.

What did the royal taster say after he drank the poisoned water?

Not much.

What's the difference between school lunch and a pile of manure?

School lunches are usually served cold.

Patient: Doctor, doctor, I've had a horrible stomachache since I ate a plate of oysters yesterday.

Doctor: Were they fresh?

Patient: I have no idea.

Doctor: How did they look when you opened the shells?

Patient: I was supposed to open the shells?

How do you make a slug drink?

Stick it in the blender.

A science teacher is teaching class. "In this bag, I have a frog, and we're going to dissect it," she says. She turns the bag over and a turkey sandwich rolls out. "That's odd," she says. "I distinctly remember eating my lunch."

DON'T EAT THAT!

Whaddaya call an unsolicited e-mail that advertises processed meat?

Spam spam.

What's green and has holes in it?

Moldy Swiss cheese.

How do you do an impression of a bird?

Eat a worm.

Why do lions eat raw meat?

Because they don't know how to cook.

Foods not eaten on the *Titanic*: Life Savers and root beer floats.

DON'T EAT THAT!

When is a slug a vegetable?

After you squash it.

What do pigs eat on hot days?

Slopsicles.

What's the worst thing in the school cafeteria?

The food.

Why was the sword swallower arrested?

He coughed and killed two people.

DON'T EAT THAT!

What's grosser than finding a worm in your apple?

Finding half a worm.

What did the Komodo dragon say when it saw a flock of turkeys?

"Gobble! Gobble!"

What's the difference between a slug and a peanut butter sandwich?

Slugs don't stick to the roof of your mouth.

What tastes worse than grape jam?

Toe jam.

DON'T EAT THAT!

Why do vultures prefer bad restaurants?

The food is rotten.

What's the difference between a grasshopper and an éclair?

A grasshopper has more cream filling.

What is the difference between school lunch and a pile of slugs?

School lunch comes on a plate.

Did you hear about the dog who ate garlic?

His bark was worse than his bite.

DON'T EAT THAT!

What do ants like on their pizza?

Antchovies.

What's gray and furry on the inside and white on the outside?

A mouse sandwich.

What happens to a daddy longlegs when it hides in a salad?

It becomes a daddy shortlegs.

What's the difference between head lice and dandruff?

Head lice are crunchier.

DON'T EAT THAT!

What happens if you eat yeast and shoe polish before bed?

You'll rise and shine in the morning.

What's the difference between a worm and a cookie?

A worm doesn't fall apart when you dunk it in milk.

Why did the boy eat the firefly?

He wanted a light snack.

What's the hardest vegetable to swallow?

The artichoke.

DON'T EAT THAT!

How do lunch ladies keep flies out of the cafeteria?

They let them taste the food.

Why should you finish your plate when you eat school lunch?

So it won't be someone else's lunch tomorrow.

How are roaches like raisins?

They both show up in oatmeal.

Mommy! Mommy! What happened to all your scabs?

Be quiet and finish your corn flakes.

DON'T EAT THAT!

Why did the dog go to school at lunchtime?

He was part of the flea lunch program.

Why did the witch send her pizza back?

They forgot the cockroaches again.

Why don't dinosaurs eat at Burger King?

They have it their way wherever they eat!

What happens if you cross a cheeseburger with a yo-yo?

After you eat it, it comes back up again.

DON'T EAT THAT!

What do you get if you swallow plutonium?

Atomic ache.

Why did dinosaurs eat other dinosaurs?

Because it takes one to gnaw one.

What do you get if you cross barf with pasta?

Ralph-i-oli.

What's the best thing they've ever had in the school cafeteria?

A fire drill.

DON'T EAT THAT!

Can you define bacteria?

It's the rear entrance to the
school cafeteria.

**What happened when they threw out
the school cafeteria leftovers?**

The alley cats threw them back.

What do you get if you eat prune pizza?

Pizzeria.

**How can you tell a mouse from
spaghetti?**

A mouse won't slip off your fork.

DON'T EAT THAT!

Why are frogs always so happy?

Because they eat whatever
bugs them.

How do you make a cockroach float?

Throw it in a root beer and add two
scoops of ice cream.

Why are false teeth like the stars?

Because they come out at night.

**Why did the lunch lady put her thumb
on the student's hamburger?**

She didn't want it to fall on the
floor again.

What kind of fish don't swim?

Dead ones.

How much money does a skunk have?

One scent.

Why was the man fired from the zoo for feeding the penguins?

Because he fed them to the lions.

What lies on the ground 100 feet up in the air?

A dead centipede.

What's grosser than a three-headed spider with 40 eyes?

Not much.

A three-legged dog walks into an Old West saloon. He sidles up to the bar and says, "I'm looking for the man who shot my paw."

CREATURE FEATURE

Where does a bee sit?

On its bee-hind.

What do you do if you find a boa constrictor in your toilet?

Wait until it's finished.

What do you get if you cross a Rottweiler and a St. Bernard?

A dog that bites off your arm and then goes for help.

What do you call a smelly sheep?

Ewwwwwe.

What goes *snap, crackle, pop*?

A dying firefly.

What do you call fishing if you don't catch any fish?

Drowning worms.

Why couldn't the vulture fly with two dead raccoons?

The plane only allowed one carrion per passenger.

What has five legs?

A lion carrying leftovers.

CREATURE FEATURE

What's black and white and flat?

A penguin flattened by a steamroller.

**What do you get when you cross a pig
with a centipede?**

Bacon and legs.

**What do you get when you cross a
T. rex with a dog?**

Something that drinks out of any toilet
it wants to.

Birdy, birdy in the sky,
Dropped some white stuff in my eye.
I'm too big to whine or cry,
I'm just glad that cows don't fly!

CREATURE FEATURE

What has 50 legs but can't walk?

Half a centipede.

What do you get if you cross a bird with a cat?

A cat that isn't hungry anymore.

What's the last thing to go through a bug's mind when it hits the windshield?

Its backside.

Two lions played poker for a giraffe.

Why were they nervous?

The game was for high steaks.

Did you hear about the fly who put himself on the map?

He got squashed in an atlas.

What do you get when you cross a pig with a comedian?

Slopstick humor.

What goes "Eek-eek! Bang!"?

A mouse riding a firework.

Why didn't the veterinarian want to treat the toad?

She was afraid it would croak.

CREATURE FEATURE

Why did the hen wash the chick's mouth out with soap?

He was using fowl language.

What's black and white and red all over?

An exploding zebra.

What do you call a bug that has worked its way to the top?

Head lice.

What's small, gray, sucks blood, and eats cheese?

A mouse-quito.

CREATURE FEATURE

What does a Triceratops sit on?

Its Tricerabottom.

**What's black and white and red
all over?**

A skunk with diaper rash.

Which reptile lives in the Emerald City?

The Lizard of Oz.

**How do you stop an octopus from
punching you?**

Disarm it.

CREATURE FEATURE

What's yellow, wiggly, and dangerous?

A maggot with a bad attitude.

What does a boa constrictor call its dinner date?

Dessert.

Why did the girl toss a snail out the window?

She wanted to see slime fly.

Little Skunk: Can I have a chemistry set for my birthday?

Skunk Mom: No way! You'll stink up the house!

CREATURE FEATURE

Why did the chicken take a bath?

It smelled fowl.

What happened to the man who tried to cross a lion with a goat?

He had to get a new goat.

What do you say when you meet a toad?

Warts new?

What's black and white and green all over?

A seasick zebra.

CREATURE FEATURE

What do you call a toothless bear?

A gummy bear.

What does a chicken say when it lays a square egg?

Ouch.

What do you call a frog with no back legs?

Unhoppy.

Why did John bring his skunk to school?

For show and smell.

18

YES WE CANNIBAL

Why do cannibals like weddings?

They get to toast the bride and groom.

What do cannibals call skateboarders?

Meals on wheels.

Did you hear about the cannibal lion with the big ego?

He had to swallow his pride.

Cannibal Kid: Dad, why can't I play with other kids?

Cannibal Dad: It's not polite to play with your food.

Why should you never upset a cannibal?

You'll end up in hot water.

How did the cannibal like his guests?

Medium well.

Cannibal Kid: Dad, I hate my math teacher.

Cannibal Dad: Then just eat your salad.

Why was the cannibal expelled from school?

She was caught buttering up the teacher.

Two explorers are walking through the forest when they get into an argument and start hitting each other. A cannibal who is spying on them yells, "Food fight!"

What's yellow and smells like people?

Cannibal barf.

Did you hear about the cannibal who thought he was a termite?

He only ate wooden legs.

What do cannibals call a bus filled with tourists?

A buffet.

Did you hear about the cannibal restaurant?

Dinner costs an arm and a leg.

Junior Cannibal: Mom! I brought a friend home for dinner.

Mommy Cannibal: Dinner is already on the table. Put your friend in the fridge and we'll have him tomorrow.

Did you hear about the cannibal who arrived late to the dinner party?

They gave him the cold shoulder.

Why did the cannibal eat the tightrope walker?

He wanted to eat a balanced diet.

What did the cannibal say to the waiter?

I'll have a large Manwich and a tossed Sally on the side.

What's a cannibal's favorite vegetable?

Human beans.

YES WE CANNIBAL

Why did the cannibal have twins in his lunch box?

Just in case he wanted seconds.

Why do cannibals make good police detectives?

Because they can really grill a suspect.

What does a cannibal eat when he's late for lunch?

Spare ribs.

What do cannibals call track stars?

Fast food.

19

THAT'S SICK

What color is a hiccup?

Burple.

What goes "Ha-ha-ha-plop!"?

Someone laughing their head off.

Doctor, doctor, what's the best way to avoid biting insects?

Quit biting them.

**There once was a lawman named Earp,
Who threw up all over some twerp.
At the OK Corral,
He said, "Sorry, pal!
I thought it was only a burp."**

Why did the fisherman go to the doctor?

He lost his herring.

What happened when the butcher backed into the meat grinder?

He got a little behind in his work.

THAT'S SICK

Why did the pig go to the eye doctor?

He had pink eye.

What do you call a person who sticks their right hand in an alligator's mouth?

Lefty.

What should you do if someone rolls their eyes at you?

Pick them up and roll them right back.

What has four legs and flies?

A dead cow.

What's green and curly?

A seasick poodle.

Mom: I thought I told you to drink your medicine after your bath.

Son: Sorry, Mom. After I finished drinking the bath, I couldn't drink another drop.

What's the difference between a peach and a wound?

One bruises easily, one oozes easily.

Nurse: The new doctor is really amusing. He'll leave you in stitches.

Patient: I hope not. I only came to collect my prescription.

What's yellow, lumpy, and flies through space?

Halley's Vomit.

Patient: Doctor, doctor! My stomach hurts. I've eaten three blue billiard balls, two red billiard balls, and an orange billiard ball.

Doctor: No wonder you aren't feeling well. You aren't getting enough greens.

What was the most common illness in the Jurassic period?

Dino-sore throats!

An apple a day keeps the doctor away. An onion a day keeps everyone away!

What did the teacher say when his glass eye went down the drain?

"Oh no, I've lost another pupil."

What's the difference between a dentist and a Yankees fan?

One roots for the Yanks and the other yanks for the roots.

Doctor: What's wrong with your wife?

Husband: She thinks she's a chicken.

Doctor: How long has she been this way?

Husband: For three years.

Doctor: Why didn't you call me sooner?

Husband: We needed the eggs.

What's the cure for dandruff?

Baldness.

Why did the lion throw up after eating Abraham Lincoln?

Because it's hard to keep a good man down.

Kid: Gramps? What's more important? Your money or your health?

Gramps: Your health, kiddo. Without your health, you're a goner.

Kid: Great. So can you lend me $20?

Fight air pollution. Gargle with mouthwash!

What do you get when you combine a drawing toy with vomit?

A Retch-a-Sketch.

Dentist: You've got the biggest cavity I've ever seen. You've got the biggest cavity I've ever seen.

Patient: You didn't have to say it twice.

Dentist: I didn't. That was an echo.

Why did the old man cover his mouth when he sneezed?

So his teeth wouldn't fly out.

Why don't zombies eat weathermen?

They give them wind.

Where does a one-handed man shop?

In a second-hand store.

What animal always pukes after it eats?

A yak.

**A man and a woman went on the road
with their animal impressions act.
She did the sounds, and
he did...the smells.**

**Where's the best place to save
toenail clippings?**

In a nail file.

Painful Reading: *Epic Fails!* by S. Platt

What should you give a seasick hippo?

Space.

Doctor, doctor, what's good for biting fingernails?

Very sharp teeth.

Why were the barber's hands so dirty?

No one had been in for a shampoo all day.

What do you call a sick alligator?

An ill-igator.

How did the dentist become a brain surgeon?

His hand slipped.

What happened when the boy drank 8 colas?

He burped 7-up.

How do you catch dandruff?

Shake your head over a paper bag.

Doctor, doctor! How can I stop my nose from running?

Stick your foot out and trip it.

What was Beethoven doing in his grave?

Decomposing.

What's green, sticky, and smells like eucalyptus?

Koala vomit.

What's wet, stinks, and goes *thump thump thump*?

A skunk in the dryer.

What does a sick dog say?

Barf! Barf! Barf!

How do you get kids to stop biting their toenails?

Make them wear shoes.

Doctor, doctor! What should I do about my yellow teeth?

Wear a brown tie.

What do you call the first person to discover fire?

Crispy.

What's it called when you throw up on an airplane?

Jet gag.

Did you hear the one about the foot?

It's pretty corny.

Did you hear the one about the fungus?

It grows on you.

What's yellow, lumpy, and smells like a zebra?

Lion puke.

Patient: Doc! Why can't I feel my legs?

Doctor: Because I had to amputate your hands.

Why did the mummy go to the doctor?

He was as pale as a ghost.

Who throws up more than any other little boy in the world?

Retchy Retch.

Doctor! Doctor! I swallowed a spoon!

Try to relax, and don't stir.

What's small, cuddly, and bright purple?

A koala holding its breath.

THAT'S SICK

What's the best airline to get sick on?

Spew-nited Airlines.

Why did T. rex need a bandage?

Because he had a dino-sore.

Patient: Doctor, my feet keep falling asleep.

Doctor: Try wearing loud socks.

Why did the toad cross the road?

To show everybody that he had guts.

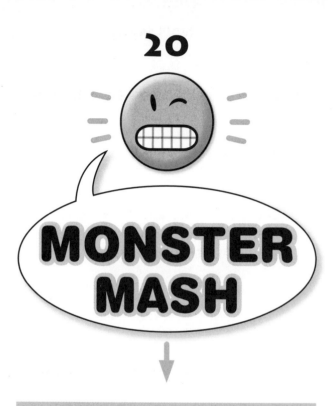

20

MONSTER MASH

Why does the mummy walk funny?

Monster wedgie.

What is Dracula's favorite fruit?

Necktarines.

MONSTER MASH

Why was the blob turned away from the restaurant?

No shirt, no shoes, no service.

Why was Dracula thrown out of the butcher shop?

He was caught chop-lifting.

Why did Death carry a broom instead of a scythe?

He wanted to be the Grim Sweeper.

What do sea monsters eat?

Fish and ships.

Why wouldn't the other little monsters play with Dracula's children?

They were vampire brats.

What do you get when you cross a vampire and a gnome?

A creature that sucks blood from your kneecaps.

Junior: Mom! Everyone at school says I look like a werewolf! Am I?

Mom: Don't be silly. Now go comb your face.

Why do vampires drink blood?

Root beer makes them burp.

What does Godzilla like to spread on his toast?

Traffic jams.

Why was Frankenstein's monster furious at his creator?

Because Dr. Frankenstein overcharged him.

I have a green nose, three red mouths, and four purple ears. What am I?

Monstrous!

Why did the vampire call the morgue?

To see if they delivered.

Little Monster: Mommy! Mommy! When is the pool going to be ready?

Momster: I don't know, but just keep spitting.

Why don't girls like Dracula?

He has bat breath.

Knock-knock!
Who's there?
Dewey.
Dewey who?
Dewey have any garlic? Dracula's at the door.

How does a monster count to 13?

On his fingers.

MONSTER MASH

What do you do with a green monster?

Put it in the sun until it ripens.

Boy Monster: Did you get the big red heart I sent you for Valentine's Day?

Girl Monster: Yes, I did. But it stopped beating. Can you send me another one?

Why do skeletons play the piano?

They don't have organs.

What do you call a 50-pound hornet with a slime gun?

Sir.

Why did the dragon burn down his own house?

He liked home cooking.

Why doesn't Death ever miss a phone call?

He has a grim beeper.

Why wouldn't the vampire eat his soup?

It had clotted.

What do you get if you cross a long-fanged, purple-spotted monster with a cat?

A town with no dogs.

Why didn't Count Dracula ever shower?

He was filthy rich.

Which monster makes the worst houseguest?

The Loch Mess Monster.

Nurse: What is your blood type?

Vampire: I'm not picky. Any type will do.

What's a vampire's favorite ice cream?

Veinilla.

What do little ghosts wear in the rain?

Ghoulashes!

How did the vampire hunters find Count Dracula's hidden lair?

He was coffin in his sleep.

Why did Frankenstein go to see a psychiatrist?

He had a screw loose.

What type of dogs do vampires like best?

Bloodhounds.

Why did the Kraken eat the pirate ship?

He wanted Cap'n Crunch for breakfast.

Which vampire liked to fly kites in thunderstorms?

Benjamin Fanglin.

Where did the skeleton keep his pet canary?

In a rib cage.

Which circus performers do vampires like best?

The jugulars.

What's a sea monster's favorite sandwich?

A sub.

21

LAST GASP

What do you call a deer with no eyes?

No eye-deer.

What do you call a deer with no eyes
and no legs?

Still no eye-deer!

242

Did you hear about the magician who likes to include his siblings in his act?

Now he has two half-sisters and one half-brother.

What's the most violent job?

Chef—because they beat eggs and whip cream.

What kind of ball should you never play with?

An eyeball.

Where are dead potatoes buried?

In gravy-yards.

Why is it so hard to get a job as a sword fighter?

The competition is cutthroat.

What do you call a dog with no legs?

It doesn't matter. He won't come anyway.

What do you DO with a dog with no legs?

Take him for a drag!

What do you get when you cross an alligator and a parrot?

I don't know, but if it asks for a cracker, better give it the whole box!

LAST GASP

Why did Mickey Mouse get hit in the head with a rock?

Because Donald ducked.

Did you hear about the stupid coyote?

He got stuck in a trap, chewed off three of his legs...and was still stuck.

What did the dumb bunny do when his computer froze?

He put it in the microwave.

Patient: Doc, you gotta help me! I broke my arm in two places!

Doctor: Try avoiding those places in the future.

How do you make a dumb bunny laugh on Tuesday?

Tell him a joke on Sunday.

Why did little Sammy feed birdseed to his cat?

Because that's where his canary was.

Patient: Doc, you gotta help me! When I drink hot chocolate, I get a stabbing pain in my right eye.

Doctor: Try taking the spoon out of the cup.

Favorite Western Movie: *Gunslingers with Gas* starring Wyatt Urp

What do you call a cow that just gave birth?

Decalfinated.

Why is it dangerous to do math in the jungle?

Because if you add 4 and 4, you get ate.

Did you hear about the cow that tried to jump over a barbed-wire fence?

It was an udder disaster.

Why did half a chicken cross the road?

To get to its other side.

Patient: Doc, you gotta help me! I've become invisible!

Doctor: Sorry, I can't see you now.

What did the half-man/half-bull say before going to the store?

"I'll be back in a minotaur."

Two goldfish are sitting in a tank.

One says to the other: "You drive, I'll man the guns."

What stands in the field and says "mmmmm"?

A cow with its lips glued together.

What do you call a man with a shovel in his head?

Doug.

Why do elephants stomp on people?

They like the squishy feeling between their toes.

What do you get if you cross a bird with a fan?

Shredded tweet.

Favorite Bathroom Reading:
Fifty Yards to the Outhouse by Willy Makit; Foreword by Betty Wont

What's brown and sits on a piano bench?

Beethoven's last movement.

Jo: Our new dog is like a member of the family.

Flo: I can see the resemblance!

What was the Blob's favorite drink?

Slime-ade!

When does a car really stink?

When it's full of gas.

How a pimple keeps its shape: Zitups!

Why did the skunk cross the road?

To get to the odor side.

Suzie: Dad, are worms good to eat?

Dad: Why do you ask?

Suzie: Because there was one in your salad.

What happened when the thief fell into wet cement?

He became a hardened criminal.

Why did the toilet paper roll down the mountain?

To get to the bottom.

Knock-knock!

Who's there?

One shoe.

One shoe who?

One shoe bathe every once in awhile?

What happened when the cat ate Mexican jumping beans?

Its poop jumped out of the litter box.

What do you get when you cross a whale with a sea slug?

Moby ick!

Red Riding Hood's Favorite Book:
Chased by a Wolf by Claude Bottom

Dog Owner: I think my dog has ticks. What should I do?

Veterinarian: Stop winding him.

How did the astronaut suffocate?

He farted in his space suit.

Book you'll never see:
Yellow River by I.P. Freely

What gave Godzilla a bellyache?

Someone he ate.

What shoots stuffing across the room?

A farting turkey.

What kind of monster can sit on the end of your finger?

The boogeyman.

Why didn't the viper viper nose?

Because the adder adder handkerchief.

Student: Do you have holes in your underwear?

Teacher: Of course not!

Student: Then how did you get your feet through them?

How are little brothers like laxatives?

They irritate the poop out of you.

If you enjoyed this special combination of our original two titles, turn the page!

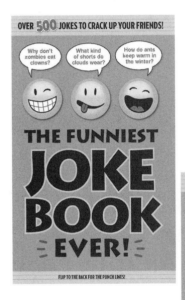

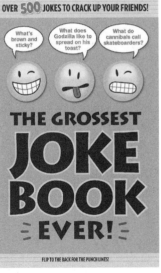

You'll be cracked up by these upcoming titles, coming to a store near you in May 2017!

The Funniest Knock-Knock Jokes Ever!
- 128 pages
- Over 358 knock-knock jokes to tell all of your friends!
- Fun for everyone ages 6 and up!

The Wackiest Joke Book Ever!
- 128 pages
- Over 476 of the silliest and wackiest jokes ever!
- Lots of laughs inside!